Editor
Mary S. Jones, M.A.

Cover Artist
Delia Rubio

Editor in Chief
Karen J. Goldfluss, M.S. Ed.

Illustrator
Greg Anderson-Clift

Art Production Manager
Kevin Barnes

Imaging
Leonard P. Swierski

Publisher

Mary D. Smith, M.S. Ed.

EARLY LANGUAGE SKILLS

Reading with Sounds

GRADES K-1

bin fin tin

- Standards-based
- Real Learning
- Really Fun!

Teacher Created Resources

TCR 8067

D1371827

Author

Hunter Calder

Teacher Created Resources, Inc.
6421 Industry Way
Westminster, CA 92683
www.teachercreated.com

ISBN: 978-1-4206-8067-6

©2008 Teacher Created Resources, Inc.
Reprint, 2012

Made in U.S.A.

Teacher Created Resources

Table of Contents

Introduction

The delightful illustrations and short, simple exercises in the *Early Language Skills* series will help young learners develop essential language skills with confidence. Each standards-based activity focuses on a specific skill. Clear instructions and examples will guide teachers and parents to help children complete the lessons successfully. Since each page includes a suggestion for extending the learning and reinforcing the skill, the books are ideal for any setting—a classroom, small-group tutoring, or at-home learning.

What's in This Book?

Once students have learned all the letters of the alphabet and can match them to their sounds, they can start putting sounds together into words. This book focuses on words that have short vowel sounds. Through using the activities in this book, students will:

- blend single-letter sounds into meaningful words
- recognize word patterns and rhymes
- match and write word patterns
- choose the correct word from a list of words with the same word patterns
- write whole words for pictures

Work actively with students through each activity so that they understand what they are expected to do on each page. Read the instructions for each activity aloud to the students and model an example. Use the certificates on the next page to reward students for their hard work after they have completed a majority of the activities.

Features of Pages

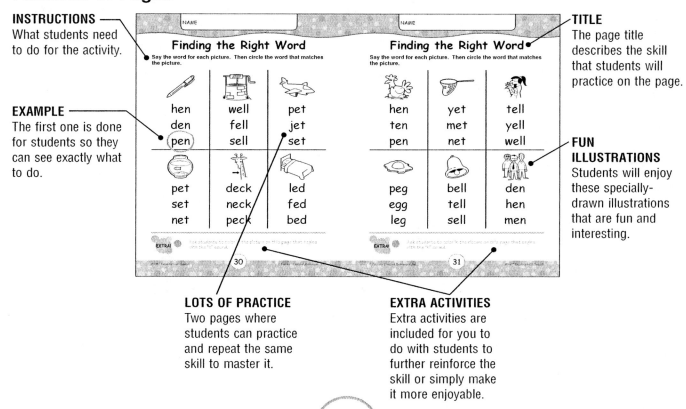

INSTRUCTIONS
What students need to do for the activity.

EXAMPLE
The first one is done for students so they can see exactly what to do.

TITLE
The page title describes the skill that students will practice on the page.

FUN ILLUSTRATIONS
Students will enjoy these specially-drawn illustrations that are fun and interesting.

LOTS OF PRACTICE
Two pages where students can practice and repeat the same skill to master it.

EXTRA ACTIVITIES
Extra activities are included for you to do with students to further reinforce the skill or simply make it more enjoyable.

This award goes to

_____

You did it!

for working so hard!

Date _____

Congratulations to

_____

for improving your language skills!

Date _____

Wow!!!

Standards and Benchmarks

The activities in this book meet the following standards, which are used with permission from McREL.

Copyright 2006 McREL. Mid-continent Research for Education and Learning.

Address: 2250 S. Parker Road, Suite 500, Aurora, CO 80014

Telephone: 303-377-0990 Website: *www.mcrel.org/standards-benchmarks*

Standard 5.   Uses the general skills and strategies of the reading process

Level I (Grades K–2)

3. Uses basic elements of phonetic analysis (e.g., common letter/sound relationships, beginning and ending consonants, vowel sounds, blends, word patterns) to decode unknown words

4. Uses basic elements of structural analysis (e.g., syllables, basic prefixes, suffixes, root words, compound words, spelling patterns, contractions) to decode unknown words

Vowel Sounds

Say each line out loud.

a as in

O as in

e as in

U as in

i as in

 **EXTRA!** It is important that students learn these sounds. Use these pages to practice beginning sounds if students are having difficulty.

6

Consonant Sounds

Say each line out loud.

b as in

g as in

c as in

h as in

d as in

j as in

f as in

 **EXTRA!** Ask students to think about what other things would match these letter sounds.

Consonant Sounds

Say each line out loud.

k as in

p as in

l as in

q as in

m as in

r as in

n as in

EXTRA! Ask students to point to the picture that ends with the "p" sound.

Consonant Sounds

Say each line out loud.

S as in

X as in

t as in

Y as in

V as in

Z as in

W as in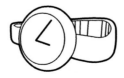

 **EXTRA!** *Students can color in the pictures.*

Matching Pictures to Words

Say the word for each picture. Then draw a line from each picture to its matching word.

fan   bag   tack   can

- -

sack   hat   cap   van

EXTRA!   Ask students to color in the pictures on this page that end with the "n" sound.

Matching Pictures to Words

Say the word for each picture. Then draw a line from each picture to its matching word.

cat　　　fan　　　rat　　　man

bat　　　pan　　　mat　　　sad

 **EXTRA!** Ask students to circle the words on this page that end with the "t" sound.

Finding the Right Word

Say the word for each picture. Then draw a line to the word that matches the picture.

	cat hat rat		lack sack pack
	ran fan man		mat fat bat
	nap gap cap		pan tan van

 **EXTRA!**   Ask students to color in the pictures on this page that begin with the "c" sound.

Finding the Right Word

Say the word for each picture. Then draw a line to the word that matches the picture.

cat	rap
sat	map
hat	sap

tack	rag
sack	tag
back	bag

tan	rat
can	sat
fan	mat

 **EXTRA!** Ask students to color in the picture on this page that begins with the "h" sound.

Finding the Right Word

Say the word for each picture. Then circle the word that matches the picture.

bat (mat) cat	pan ran tan	van tan fan
sack rack back	pan can man	had sad bad

EXTRA! Ask students to color in the picture on this page that begins with the "p" sound.

#8067 Reading with Sounds

Finding the Right Word

Say the word for each picture. Then circle the word that matches the picture.

fat	can	lap
bat	ban	tap
sat	ran	map
ran	flag	jam
van	drag	ram
man	brag	ham

 **EXTRA!** Ask students to color in the picture on this page that begins with the "b" sound.

Writing Same Spelling Patterns

Say the word for each picture. Trace over the word for the picture, then write two more words with the same word pattern.

r <u>a</u> <u>t</u>

f _ _

v _ _

b <u>a</u> <u>g</u>

t _ _

r _ _

c <u>a</u> <u>n</u>

m _ _

p _ _

s <u>a</u> <u>d</u>

m _ _

b _ _

EXTRA! Ask students to think of other words with these same spelling patterns.

Writing Same Spelling Patterns

Say the word for each picture. Trace over the word for the picture, then write two more words with the same word pattern.

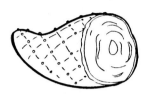

h <u>a m</u>

j _ _

r _ _

v <u>a</u> n

c _ _

t _ _

h <u>a t</u>

r _ _

s _ _

t <u>a c k</u>

s _ _ _

b _ _ _

EXTRA!

Ask students to circle the words on this page that begin with the "r" sound.

(17)

Matching Words With Same Spelling Patterns

Say the words in each box. Then draw a line between the words with the same word pattern or ending.

man	tap
bag	ran
map	sag

sack	jab
cab	bad
sad	rack

wag	pad
sat	tag
mad	mat

fat	wax
ran	pat
tax	van

EXTRA! Ask students to circle the words on this page that rhyme with "hat."

Matching Words With Same Spelling Patterns

Say the words in each box. Then draw a line between the words with the same word pattern or ending.

back	tan
rap	tack
pan	map

ram	can
fan	hat
bat	dam

rag	ram
lack	lag
jam	sack

nab	lad
pat	cat
dad	tab

 **EXTRA!**   Ask students to circle the words that rhyme with "pack."

Writing Words

Say the word for each picture. Then write the word for the picture on the line.

 fan  _____

 _____  _____

 _____ _____

 _____  _____

 **EXTRA!** Ask students to color in the pictures on this page that rhyme with "sat."

Writing Words

Say the word for each picture. Then write the word for the picture on the line.

 _____

 _____

 _____

 _____

 _____

 _____

 _____

 _____

EXTRA! Ask students to color in the pictures on this page that rhyme with "ran."

Making Words

Say the sounds in each box. Write the sounds in the spaces provided. Then read the words aloud.

v + a + n = | v | a | n |

s + a + d =

t + a + g =

j + a + m =

c + a + p =

s + a + t =

EXTRA! Make up or purchase a set of cards with one letter on each. Students can practice putting the letters together to make words.

22

©Teacher Created Resources, Inc.

Making Words

Say the sounds in each box. Write the sounds in the spaces provided. Then read the words aloud.

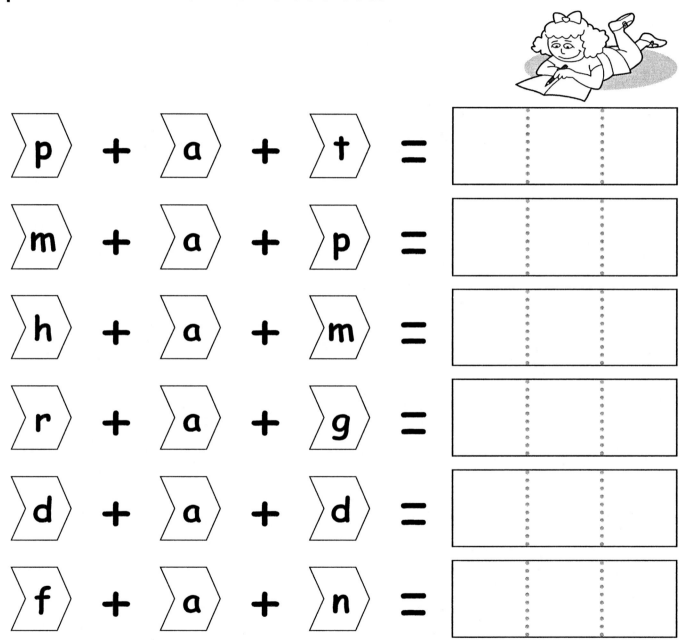

p + a + t =

m + a + p =

h + a + m =

r + a + g =

d + a + d =

f + a + n =

EXTRA!

Using a set of single-letter cards, show students a picture of a simple object (e.g., bag, hat) and ask them to make up the word using the cards.

        #8067 Reading with Sounds

Fitting the Right Word

Read the words in each group. Write the word that has the right shape to fit inside the boxes.

mad   fan   bag
pad   pan   sag
dad   can   rag

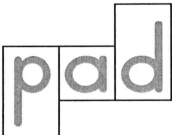
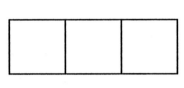
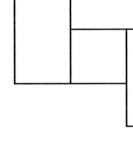

jam   tap
ham   gap
ram   cap

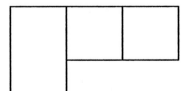
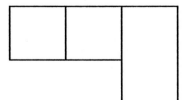

EXTRA!

This activity requires understanding of the shape of letters. Can students point to all the "tall" letters on the page (e.g., d, h)?

Fitting the Right Word

Read the words in each group. Write the word that has the right shape to fit inside the boxes.

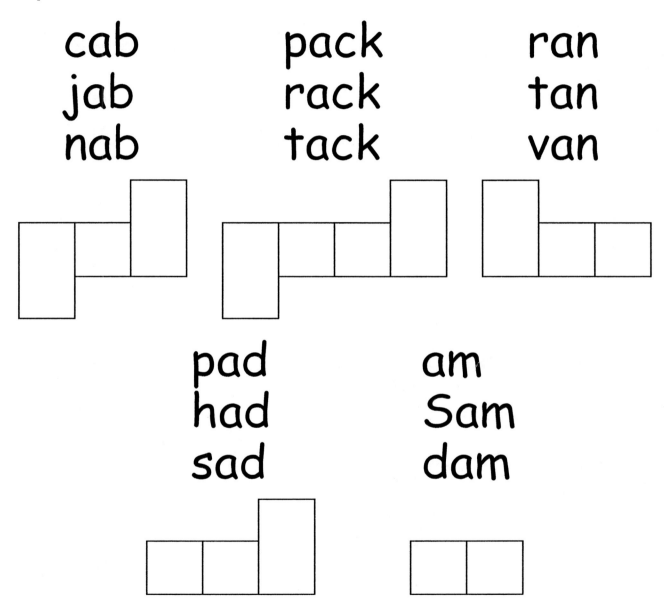

cab
jab
nab

pack
rack
tack

ran
tan
van

pad
had
sad

am
Sam
dam

 **EXTRA!** Draw similar boxes on a sheet of paper or on the board and ask students to fit in a word that they know.

25

Matching Pictures to Words

Say the word for each picture. Then draw a line from each picture to its matching word.

ten   web   net   egg

- -

leg   bed   well   neck

EXTRA! Ask students to find the picture on this page that rhymes with "red" and color it in red.

Matching Pictures to Words

Say the word for each picture. Then draw a line from each picture to its matching word.

jet   men   pen   bell

      10

pet   ten   yell   hen

EXTRA!  Ask students to find the picture on this page that begins with the "y" sound. What color starts with a "y" sound? Then ask students to color the picture in that "y" color.

Finding the Right Word

Say the word for each picture. Then draw a line to the word that matches the picture.

fell
sell
bell

den
ten
pen

peg
leg
beg

bed
fed
led

wet
set
net

deck
neck
peck

EXTRA! Making simple word cards can help students recognize whole words. Cut out matching pictures from magazines, or draw simple pictures on cards, then help students match them up to the word cards.

28

©Teacher Created Resources, Inc.

Finding the Right Word

Say the word for each picture. Then draw a line to the word that matches the picture.

sell

yell

tell

den

pen

hen

men

ten

pen

let

wet

jet

bell

tell

well

10

ten

pen

hen

EXTRA!   *Students can color in the pictures.*

Finding the Right Word

Say the word for each picture. Then circle the word that matches the picture.

hen den (pen)	well fell sell	pet jet set
pet set net	deck neck peck	led fed bed

EXTRA! Ask students to color in the picture on this page that begins with the "b" sound.

Finding the Right Word

Say the word for each picture. Then circle the word that matches the picture.

hen ten pen	yet met net	tell yell well

peg egg leg	bell tell sell	den hen men

 **EXTRA!** Ask students to color in the picture on this page that begins with the "h" sound.

31

Writing Same Spelling Patterns

Say the word for each picture. Trace over the word for the picture, then write two more words with the same word pattern.

b <u>e d</u>

r _ _

f _ _

n <u>e t</u>

b _ _

l _ _

l <u>e g</u>

p _ _

b _ _

h <u>e n</u>

d _ _

m _ _

Ask students to color in the picture on this page that begins with the "b" sound.

Writing Same Spelling Patterns

Say the word for each picture. Trace over the word for the picture, then write two more words with the same word pattern.

m _e_ n

p _ _

d _ _

w _e_ t

p _ _

j _ _

b _e_ l l

t _ _ _

s _ _ _

n _e_ c k

d _ _ _

p _ _ _

EXTRA! Ask students to find the picture on this page that rhymes with "spell."

Matching Words With Same Spelling Patterns

Say the words in each box. Then draw a line between the words with the same word pattern or ending.

den	red
fed	let
get	hen

sell	mess
leg	fell
less	beg

deck	led
pen	peck
wed	men

pet	leg
tell	well
peg	met

 **EXTRA!**   How many words on this page rhyme with "ten"? Ask students to circle them, then count them.

34

Matching Words With Same Spelling Patterns

Say the words in each box. Then draw a line between the words with the same word pattern or ending.

ten	fed
bed	den
set	wet

tell	neck
yet	fell
peck	let

net	pen
red	pet
men	fed

leg	net
yell	beg
met	bell

EXTRA! How many words on this page rhyme with "get"? Ask students to circle them, then count them.

Writing Words

Say the word for each picture. Then write the word for the picture on the line.

_____

_____   _____

_____   _____

_____   _____

EXTRA!   Before writing in each word, ask students to say each sound they can hear aloud, then write in the sounds as they say them.

Writing Words

Say the word for each picture. Then write the word for the picture on the line.

 _____

 _____

 _____

 _____

 _____

10 _____

 _____

 _____

EXTRA!

Which word on this page starts with the "b" sound?
Ask students to color it in blue.

Making Words

Say the sounds in each box. Write the sounds in the spaces provided. Then read the words aloud.

>d⟩ + >e⟩ + >n⟩ = | d | e | n |

>r⟩ + >e⟩ + >d⟩ =

>n⟩ + >e⟩ + >t⟩ =

>l⟩ + >e⟩ + >g⟩ =

>m⟩ + >e⟩ + >n⟩ =

>y⟩ + >e⟩ + >s⟩ =

 **EXTRA!** Having a magnetic set of alphabet letters on the board is a great way to help students become more familiar with letters.

(38)

Making Words

Say the sounds in each box. Write the sounds in the spaces provided. Then read the words aloud.

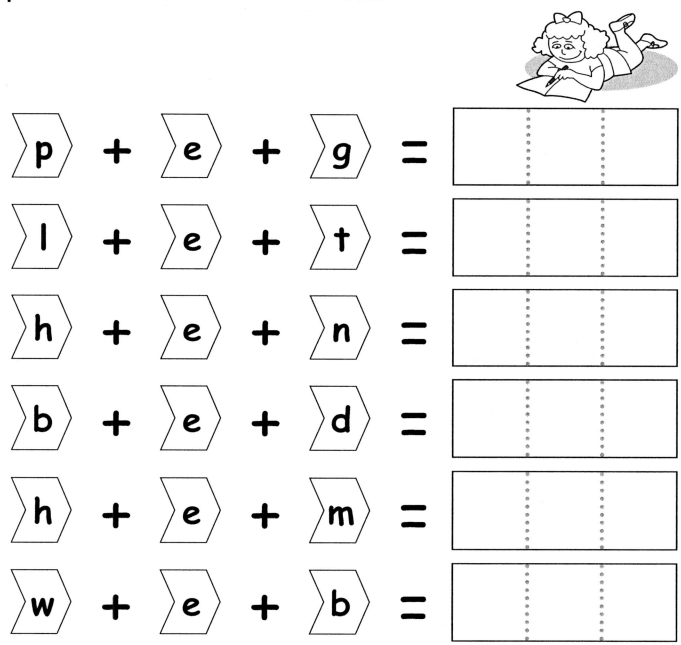

$$p + e + g =$$

$$l + e + t =$$

$$h + e + n =$$

$$b + e + d =$$

$$h + e + m =$$

$$w + e + b =$$

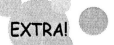

EXTRA! Ask students to write each word on this page again on an erasable writing surface or on a sheet of paper.

Fitting the Right Word

Read the words in each group. Write the word that has the right shape to fit inside the boxes.

den
ten
pen

fed
red
led

bet
let
get

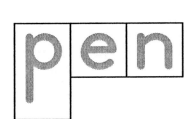

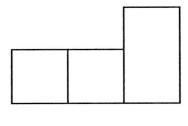

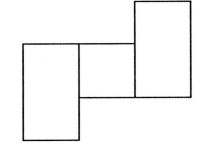

beg
leg
peg

less
mess
yes

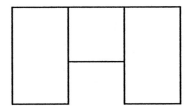

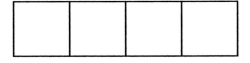

EXTRA! How many words on this page rhyme with "dress"?
Ask students to circle them.

©Teacher Created Resources, Inc.

Fitting the Right Word

Read the words in each group. Write the word that has the right shape to fit inside the boxes.

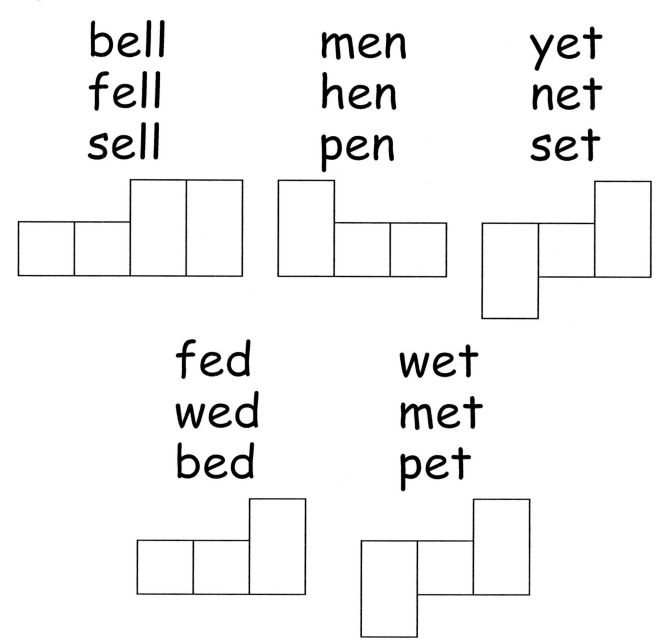

bell
fell
sell

men
hen
pen

yet
net
set

fed
wed
bed

wet
met
pet

EXTRA!

How many words on this page rhyme with "get"?
Ask students to circle them.

Matching Pictures to Words

Say the word for each picture. Then draw a line from each picture to its matching word.

dig   hill   lick   six

lips   zip   big   pin

 **EXTRA!**   Help students think of other words with the "i" sound by giving them clues, e.g., "What goes on top of a pot?" (lid).

Matching Pictures to Words

Say the word for each picture. Then draw a line from each picture to its matching word.

pig   wig   kiss   bin

kick   bib   sick   fin

 **EXTRA!**   Ask students to find the picture on this page that rhymes with "tin."

#8067 Reading with Sounds

Finding the Right Word

Say the word for each picture. Then draw a line to the word that matches the picture.

lip			fill
zip			bill
tip			pill
wig			bin
rig			fin
big			tin
wick			big
tick			fig
kick			dig

EXTRA! Help students think of other words with the "–in" word pattern sound by giving them clues, e.g., "What do you do when you turn around and around" (spin) or "What's at the bottom of your face?" (chin).

44

Finding the Right Word

Say the word for each picture. Then draw a line to the word that matches the picture.

sick
pick
lick

pig
fig
wig

fill
will
hill

6

six
fix
mix

bit
sit
fit

rib
fib
bib

EXTRA!

Ask students to circle the words on this page that begin with the "p" sound.

Finding the Right Word

Say the word for each picture. Then circle the word that matches the picture.

tin (pin) win	zip lip rip	big fig dig
bib rib nib	tips dips lips	six mix fix

 **EXTRA!** Ask students to color in the picture on this page that begins with the "d" sound.

Finding the Right Word

Say the word for each picture. Then circle the word that matches the picture.

bit fit hit	bin win pin	big wig dig
kiss miss hiss	kick lick tick	hit pit sit

EXTRA! Ask students to color in the picture on this page that begins with the "w" sound.

#8067 Reading with Sounds

Writing Same Spelling Patterns

Say the word for each picture. Trace over the word for the picture, then write two more words with the same word pattern.

h _i_ _l_ _l_

b _ _ _ _

f _ _ _ _

z _i_ _p_

l _ _ _

t _ _ _

b _i_ _g_

w _ _ _

f _ _ _

b _i_ _n_

w _ _ _

p _ _ _

 **EXTRA!** Ask students to match up a set of simple word cards with some pictures, then write each word on a piece of paper.

48

Writing Same Spelling Patterns

Say the word for each picture. Trace over the word for the picture, then write two more words with the same word pattern.

6

s _i_ _t_

b _ _ _

f _ _ _

s _i_ _x_

m _ _ _

f _ _ _

b _i_ _b_

r _ _ _

f _ _ _

l _i_ _c_ _k_

s _ _ _ _

k _ _ _ _

EXTRA! Ask students to color in the picture on this page that rhymes with "stick."

Matching Words With Same Spelling Patterns

Say the words in each box. Then draw a line between the words with the same word pattern or ending.

wick	mill
fill	kiss
miss	lick

bin	lip
pick	wick
nip	win

hid	fix
rim	lid
mix	dim

bit	rib
will	hit
bib	pill

EXTRA!

How many words on this page rhyme with "tip"? Ask students to circle them, then count them.

50

Matching Words With Same Spelling Patterns

Say the words in each box. Then draw a line between the words with the same word pattern or ending.

bid	fit
him	rid
kit	rim

fill	mix
pin	will
six	tin

sick	dim
did	tick
rim	kid

fib	dig
tip	dip
pig	bib

 **EXTRA!** How many words on this page rhyme with "swim"? Ask students to circle them, then count them.

51

Writing Words

Say the word for each picture. Then write the word for the picture on the line.

 ___fin___

 _____

 _____

 _____

 _____

 _____

6 _____

 _____

EXTRA! Using simple word puzzles or alphabet blocks to help students form words is a great way to help them retain information. The more often they use and manipulate letters and sounds, the easier it will be for them to learn new words.

Writing Words

Say the word for each picture. Then write the word for the picture on the line.

 _____

 _____

  _____

 _____

  _____

 _____

Making Words

Say the sounds in each box. Write the sounds in the spaces provided. Then read the words aloud.

| m | + | i | + | x | = | m | i | x |

| b | + | i | + | b | = | | | |

| k | + | i | + | t | = | | | |

| d | + | i | + | p | = | | | |

| w | + | i | + | n | = | | | |

| h | + | i | + | m | = | | | |

EXTRA! Ask students to color in the blocks on this page that have the "m" sound.

#8067 Reading with Sounds

Making Words

Say the sounds in each box. Write the sounds in the spaces provided. Then read the words aloud.

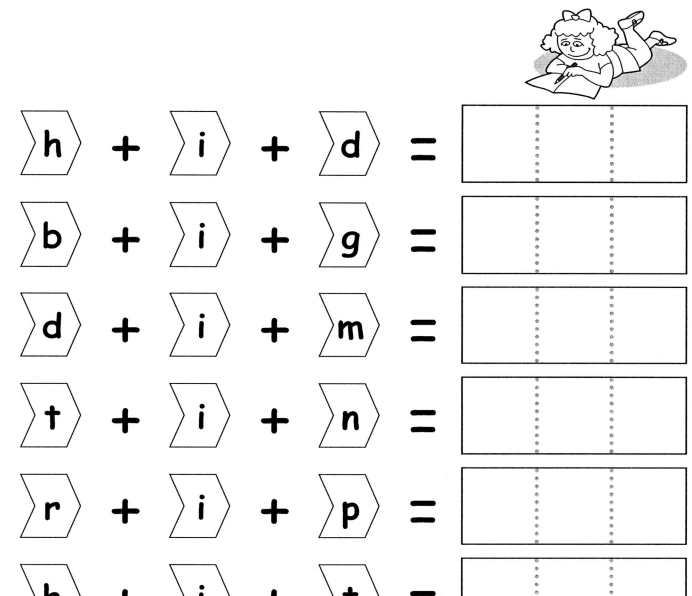

h + i + d =

b + i + g =

d + i + m =

t + i + n =

r + i + p =

h + i + t =

EXTRA! Ask students to color in the blocks on this page that have the "d" sound.

Fitting the Right Word

Read the words in each group. Write the word that has the right shape to fit inside the boxes.

rid
hid
lid

big
wig
dig

nip
hip
lip

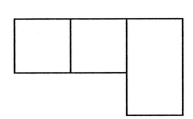

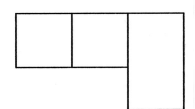

bin
pin
tin

dim
him
rim

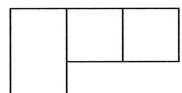

EXTRA!  How many words on this page rhyme with "pip"? Help students think of more rhyming words.

Fitting the Right Word

Read the words in each group. Write the word that has the right shape to fit inside the boxes.

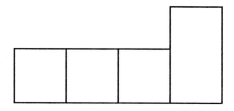

kick
sick
lick

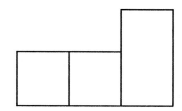

rib
bib
fib

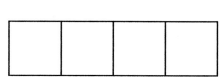

miss
hiss
kiss

mix
six
fix

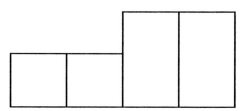

pill
will
hill

EXTRA!

How many words on this page rhyme with "spill"? Ask students to circle them.

Matching Pictures to Words

Say the word for each picture. Then draw a line from each picture to its matching word.

lock   ox   top   doll

box   sock   log   mop

EXTRA!

Help students think of other words with the "o" sound by giving them clues, eg., "What tells the time?" (clock) or "What animal is green and lives in a pond?" (frog).

Matching Pictures to Words

Say the word for each picture. Then draw a line from each picture to its matching word.

hop   fox   rock   dog

- -

cob   jog   sob   pot

 **EXTRA!** Ask students to color in the pictures on this page that rhyme with "log."

Finding the Right Word

Say the word for each picture. Then draw a line to the word that matches the picture.

jog
log
dog

sod
pod
rod

rock
sock
dock

fox
box
pox

pop
mop
hop

job
mob
sob

 **EXTRA!**   Ask students to color in the picture on this page with the "—ock" word pattern.

60

Finding the Right Word

Say the word for each picture. Then draw a line to the word that matches the picture.

mop
hop
top

top
cop
pop

lock
rock
sock

ox
fox
box

hot
not
pot

sob
cob
rob

 **EXTRA!**

Ask students to color in the picture on this page with the "–ox" word pattern.

Finding the Right Word

Say the word for each picture. Then circle the word that matches
the picture.

fog hog (log)	doll roll toll	top mop hop
dog jog log	rod pod nod	not hot pot

EXTRA! You could try this activity using cards with simple words written
on them that match up with pictures cut from magazines.

Finding the Right Word

Say the word for each picture. Then circle the word that matches the picture.

box	hop	rock
ox	lop	dock
fox	top	lock
sob	rock	jog
job	sock	log
cob	lock	dog

EXTRA! Ask students to color in the picture on this page that begins with the "s" sound.

63

Writing Same Spelling Patterns

Say the word for each picture. Trace over the word for the picture, then write two more words with the same word pattern.

h <u>o</u> <u>p</u>

t _ _

m _ _

c <u>o</u> <u>b</u>

s _ _

j _ _

l <u>o</u> <u>g</u>

j _ _

d _ _

p <u>o</u> <u>d</u>

r _ _

n _ _

EXTRA! Ask students to color in the picture on this page that rhymes with "dog."

Writing Same Spelling Patterns

Say the word for each picture. Trace over the word for the picture, then write two more words with the same word pattern.

p <u>o t</u>

d _ _

c _ _

j <u>o g</u>

l _ _

f _ _

t <u>o p</u>

p _ _

h _ _

r <u>o c k</u>

s _ _ _

l _ _ _

EXTRA!

Ask students to color in the picture on this page that rhymes with "mop."

Matching Words With Same Spelling Patterns

Say the words in each box. Then draw a line between the words with the same word pattern or ending.

boss	job
on	loss
mob	Ron

mock	got
jog	fog
not	rock

nod	pop
log	pod
top	dog

bob	cod
mop	sob
rod	hop

EXTRA! How many words on this page rhyme with "stop"? Ask students to circle them, then count them.

66

Matching Words With Same Spelling Patterns

Say the words in each box. Then draw a line between the words with the same word pattern or ending.

sob	rod
ox	cob
pod	box

pot	job
lob	cot
dog	bog

cop	rock
fox	box
lock	hop

loss	hot
dot	dock
sock	toss

EXTRA!   How many words on this page rhyme with "not"? Ask students to circle them, then count them.

Writing Words

Say the word for each picture. Then write the word for the picture on the line.

  cob

 **EXTRA!** Before writing in each word, ask students to say each sound they can hear aloud, then write in the sounds as they say them.

Writing Words

Say the word for each picture. Then write the word for the picture on the line.

 _____

 _____

 _____

 _____

 _____

 _____

 _____

 _____

EXTRA! Which word on this page starts with the "r" sound? Ask students to color it in red.

Making Words

Say the sounds in each box. Write the sounds in the spaces provided. Then read the words aloud.

m + o + b = m o b

r + o + d =

l + o + g =

t + o + p =

g + o + t =

b + o + x =

EXTRA! Ask students to color in the blocks on this page that have the "b" sound in blue.

©Teacher Created Resources, Inc.

Making Words

Say the sounds in each box. Write the sounds in the spaces provided. Then read the words aloud.

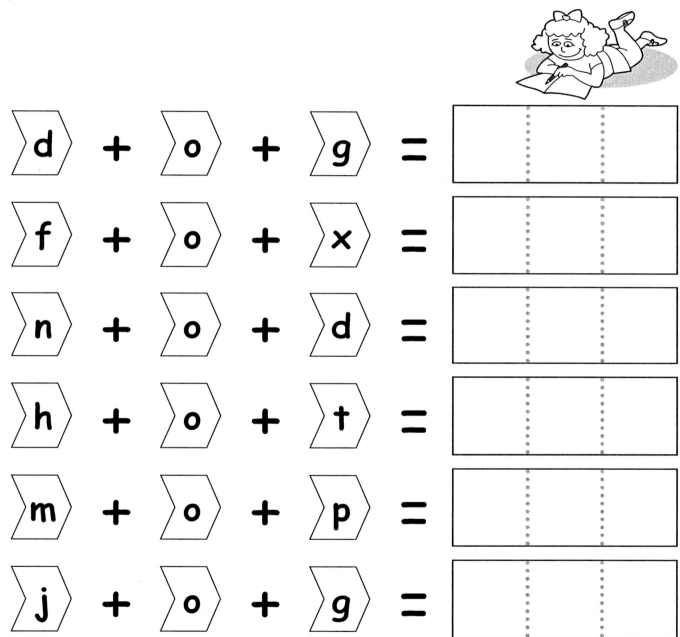

d + o + g =

f + o + x =

n + o + d =

h + o + t =

m + o + p =

j + o + g =

EXTRA! Ask students to color the blocks on this page that have the "g" sound in green.

Fitting the Right Word

Read the words in each group. Write the word that has the right shape to fit inside the boxes.

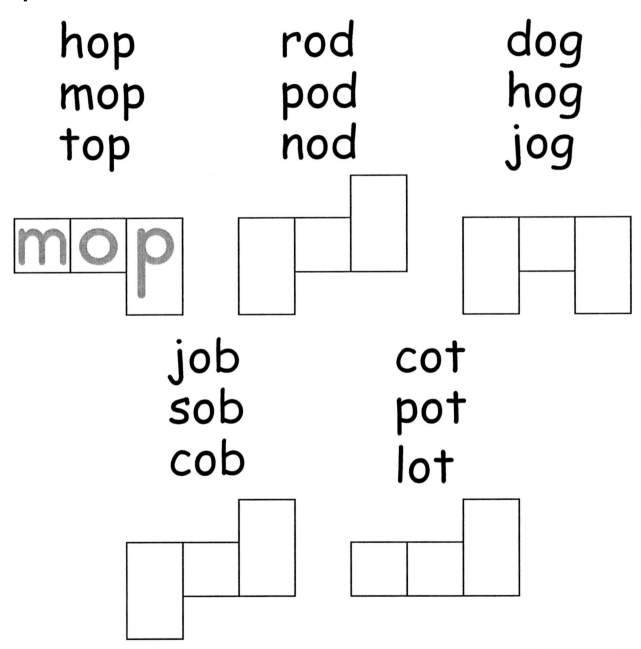

hop
mop
top

rod
pod
nod

dog
hog
jog

job
sob
cob

cot
pot
lot

 **EXTRA!**

Ask students to write each word again on a separate sheet of paper. Concentrate on helping them see which letters are the "tall" ones.

(72)

©Teacher Created Resources, Inc.

Fitting the Right Word

Read the words in each group. Write the word that has the right shape to fit inside the boxes.

 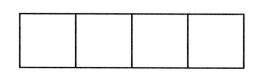 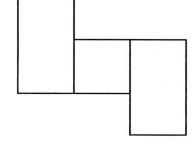

on   boss   cop
Ron   moss   pop
Don   toss   top

rock   mob
sock   lob
lock   job

 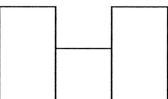

EXTRA! How many words on this page rhyme with "dock"?
Ask students to circle them.

Matching Pictures to Words

Say the word for each picture. Then draw a line from each picture to its matching word.

   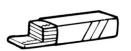

gum   jug   hug   pup

bus   cut   run   tub

 **EXTRA!**   Help students think of other words with the "u" sound by giving them clues, e.g., "What stops the water from running down the sink?" (plug) or "What noisy thing can you play with two sticks?" (drum).

Matching Pictures to Words

Say the word for each picture. Then draw a line from each picture to its matching word.

  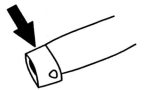 

cub   duck   cuff   mug

bug   cup   sun   gull

 **EXTRA!**   Ask students to color in the picture on this page that rhymes with "fun."

Finding the Right Word

Say the word for each picture. Then draw a line to the word that matches the picture.

tug

bug

rug

cut

hut

nut

run

sun

fun

luck

duck

tuck

up

pup

cup

mug

tug

hug

EXTRA! Ask students to color in the picture on this page with the "–up" word pattern.

Finding the Right Word

Say the word for each picture. Then draw a line to the word that matches the picture.

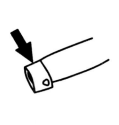
cuff
huff
puff

tub
rub
cub

run
sun
bun

gull
hull
lull

us
Gus
bus

mug
hug
tug

EXTRA!

Ask students to color in the picture on this page with the "–un" word pattern.

Finding the Right Word

Say the word for each picture. Then circle the word that matches the picture.

bug (jug) mug	cub tub rub	bun fun run
luck tuck duck	cup up pup	us bus Gus

EXTRA! Ask students to color in the picture on this page that begins with the "d" sound.

78

Finding the Right Word

Say the word for each picture. Then circle the word that matches the picture.

hug tug rug	gum bum sum	cup pup up
huff cuff puff	gull dull lull	rut nut cut

EXTRA! Ask students to color in the picture on this page that begins with the "n" sound.

Writing Same Spelling Patterns

Say the word for each picture. Trace over the word for the picture, then write two more words with the same word pattern.

t u b

r _ _

c _ _

b u g

t _ _

d _ _

s u n

b _ _

r _ _

c u t

h _ _

b _ _

EXTRA!

Ask students to color in the picture on this page that rhymes with "rub."

Writing Same Spelling Patterns

Say the word for each picture. Trace over the word for the picture, then write two more words with the same word pattern.

r <u>u</u> n

f _ _

s _ _

h <u>u</u> g

r _ _

b _ _

d <u>u c k</u>

t _ _ _

m _ _ _

g <u>u</u> l l

d _ _ _

l _ _ _

Matching Words With Same Spelling Patterns

Say the words in each box. Then draw a line between the words with the same word pattern or ending.

dull	bus
fuzz	hull
us	buzz

up	puff
huff	tuck
luck	pup

cub	hug
bug	rub
gum	hum

fun	hut
bud	run
but	mud

EXTRA! How many words on this page rhyme with "cuff"? Ask students to circle them, then count them.

82

Matching Words With Same Spelling Patterns

Say the words in each box. Then draw a line between the words with the same word pattern or ending.

tub	muck
mug	tug
duck	cub

cut	cup
lull	nut
pup	gull

lug	run
sun	jug
gum	sum

gum	luck
cuff	puff
buck	hum

 **EXTRA!**   How many words on this page rhyme with "bug"? Ask students to circle them, then count them.

Writing Words

Say the word for each picture. Then write the word for the picture on the line.

 _cub_ _____

 _____ _____

 _____ _____

 _____ _____

EXTRA!  Ask students to color in the picture on this page that ends with the "b" sound.

84

Writing Words

Say the word for each picture. Then write the word for the picture on the line.

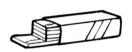 _____

 _____

  _____

  _____

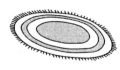 _____

  _____

 _____

 _____

EXTRA!   Ask students to color in the pictures on this page that end with the "t" sound.

Making Words

Say the sounds in each box. Write the sounds in the spaces provided. Then read the words aloud.

$$b + u + d = \boxed{b \; u \; d}$$

$$n + u + t = \boxed{}$$

$$f + u + n = \boxed{}$$

$$h + u + m = \boxed{}$$

$$r + u + b = \boxed{}$$

$$p + u + p = \boxed{}$$

EXTRA! Ask students to color the blocks on this page that have the "p" sound in purple.

Making Words

Say the sounds in each box. Write the sounds in the spaces provided. Then read the words aloud.

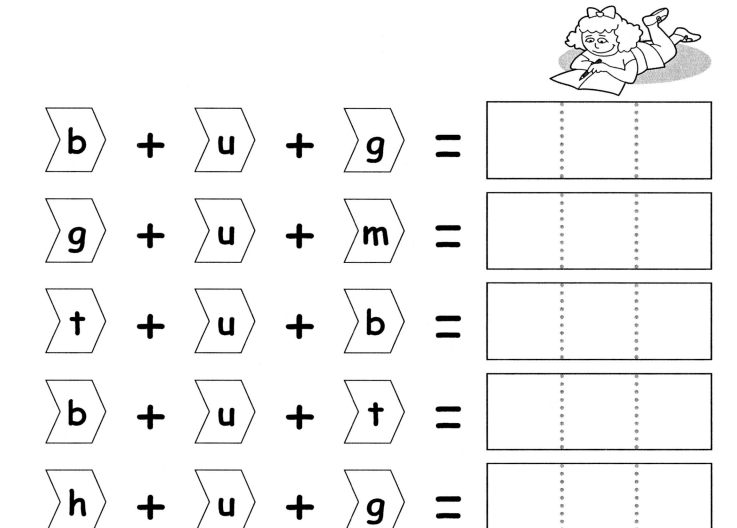

b + u + g =

g + u + m =

t + u + b =

b + u + t =

h + u + g =

s + u + n =

Write each word on this page on a separate card. Ask students to match the cards to the words they have written on the page.

©*Teacher Created Resources, Inc.*   #*8067 Reading with Sounds*

Fitting the Right Word

Read the words in each group. Write the word that has the right shape to fit inside the boxes.

rub
tub
cub

hug
dug
mug

hum
gum
sum

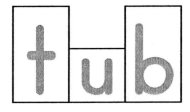

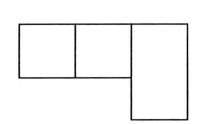

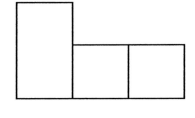

bun
fun
sun

cut
but
hut

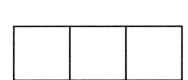

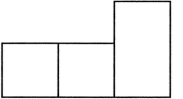

 **EXTRA!**

How many words on this page rhyme with "tug"? Ask students to circle them.

88

Fitting the Right Word

Read the words in each group. Write the word that has the right shape to fit inside the boxes.

hull
dull
gull

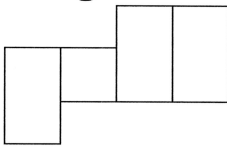

hub
cub
rub

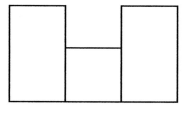

bug
jug
tug

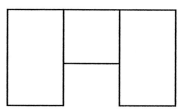

puff
huff
cuff

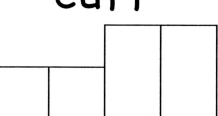

duck
muck
suck

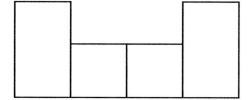

EXTRA!

How many words on this page rhyme with "tub"?
Ask students to circle them.

Matching the Right Word

Say the word for each picture. Draw a line to the correct word, then write the word in the spaces provided.

sit

sat

set

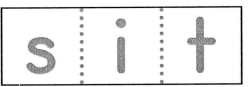
s | i | t

pin

pen

pan

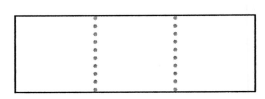

cat

cot

cut

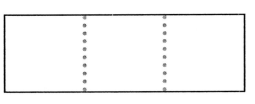

EXTRA! You could try this activity using real objects or pictures with simple names. Show students the object. Can they make the word using cards with letters on them?

90

©*Teacher Created Resources, Inc.*

Matching the Right Word

Say the word for each picture. Draw a line to the correct word, then write the word in the spaces provided.

pot

pet

pat

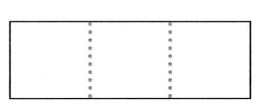

hut

hit

hat

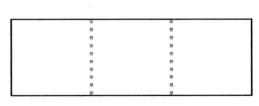

bad

bed

bud

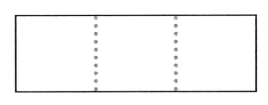

EXTRA!

Using a set of single-letter cards, help students make simple words using each of the five vowel sounds. You can help them by giving clues, such as, "What do we cook eggs in?" (pan).

Matching the Right Word

Say the word for each picture. Draw a line to the correct word, then write the word in the spaces provided.

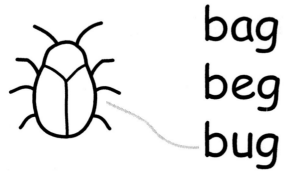

bag

beg

bug

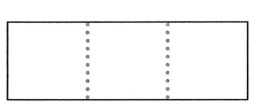

pin

pan

pen

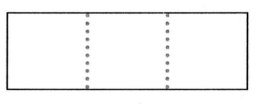

not

nut

net

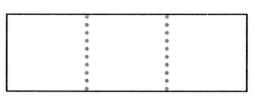

 **EXTRA!**   Ask students to circle all the words with the "e" sound.

92

Matching the Right Word

Say the word for each picture. Draw a line to the correct word, then write the word in the spaces provided.

will

well

wall

tick

tuck

tack

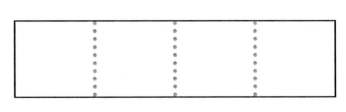

sock

suck

sick

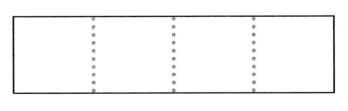

 **EXTRA!** Ask students to think about another group of words that follows this activity's pattern.

Picture Crosswords

Write the words that match the pictures in the crossword squares. The arrows will show you where to start each word.

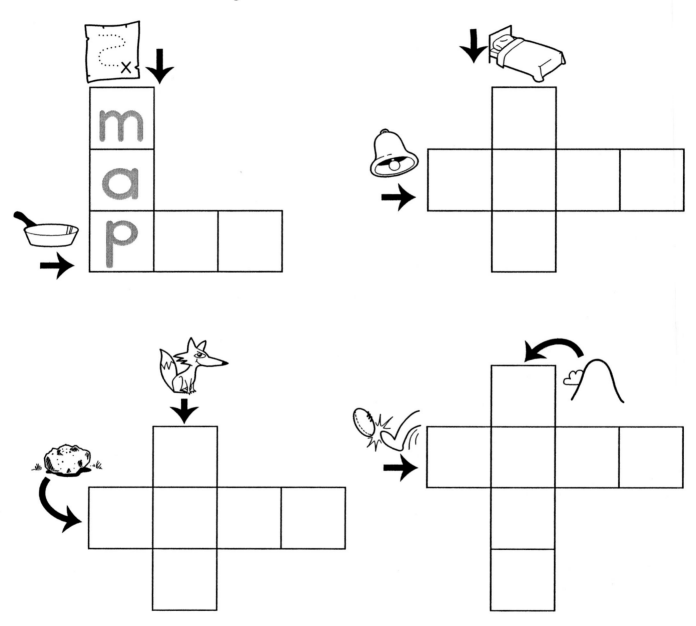

Make a set of cards with single letters on them, and help students rearrange them to make words.

Picture Crosswords

Write the words that match the pictures in the crossword squares. The arrows will show you where to start each word.

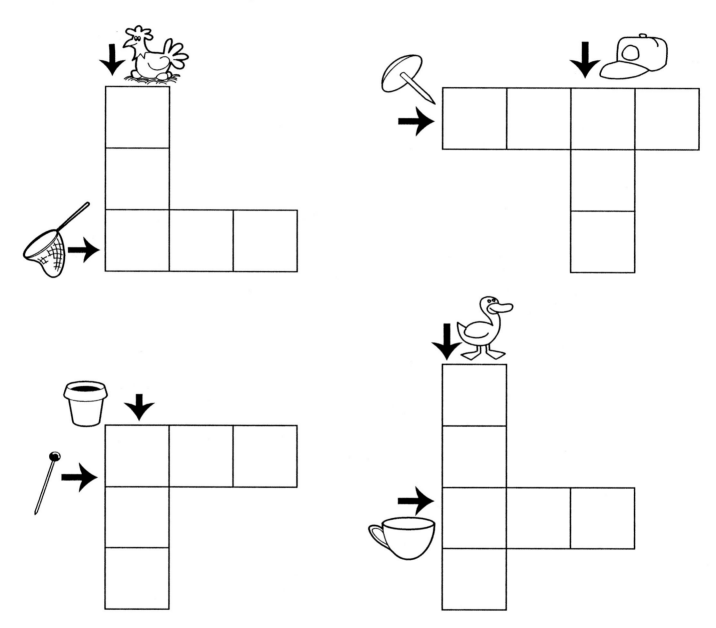

When students can read full words, encourage them to look for familiar or simple words around them in the classroom.

Picture Crosswords

Write the words that match the pictures in the crossword squares.
The arrows will show you where to start each word.

EXTRA! Ask students to try to make their own picture crosswords.